S-CLASS BY MERCEDES-BENZ

A Crabtree Branches Book

Tracy Nelson Maurer

Schoo-to-Home Support for Caregivers and Teachers

This high-interest book is designed to motivate striving students with engaging topics while building fluency, vocabulary, and an interest in reading. Here are a few questions and activities to help the reader build upon his or her comprehension skills.

Before Reading:

- *What do I think this book is about?*
- *What do I know about this topic?*
- *What do I want to learn about this topic?*
- *Why am I reading this book?*

During Reading:

- *I wonder why...*
- *I'm curious to know...*
- *How is this like something I already know?*
- *What have I learned so far?*

After Reading:

- *What was the author trying to teach me?*
- *What are some details?*
- *How did the photographs and captions help me understand more?*
- *Read the book again and look for the vocabulary words.*
- *What questions do I still have?*

Extension Activities:

- *What was your favorite part of the book? Write a paragraph on it.*
- *Draw a picture of your favorite thing you learned from the book.*

TABLE OF CONTENTS

WORLD-CLASS LUXURY

The Mercedes-Benz attitude has been "the best or nothing" since the company began in 1926. Today, the company's S-Class reigns among the world's top luxury vehicles. S-Class includes full-size cars, limousines, and armored vehicles. The S-Class **flagship** four-door sedans start at about $96,000.

In 1954, Mercedes-Benz introduced its *Sonderklass,* German for "special class." It shortened over time to S-Class.

For many years, S-Class two-door options included the **coupé** and convertible. The company made the last of these cars in 2021 to focus on more popular models.

Convertibles are called cabriolets (say: CAB ree OH lays) in many European countries. The S-Class cabriolet starts at about $185,400.

SCULPTED BEAUTY

The S-Class sedan looks like sculpted steel. The sleek design features smooth door handles that pop up when the driver stands near the door with the key fob. **Chrome** accents above the horizontal taillights and on the lower sides highlight the elegant style.

The upscale Saks Fifth Avenue store offered 20 special-edition Mercedes-Benz S600 sedans in its 2005 Christmas catalog. At $145,000 each, they were sold out in less than seven minutes.

Redesigned in 2021, the S-Class sedan measures 1.3 inches (3.3 cm) longer and 2 inches (5 cm) wider than earlier models. This adds passenger and trunk space.

The S500 and S580 models available in the U.S. come with 4Matic all-wheel drive for road-hugging control.

Mercedes-Benz developed E-Active Body Control with an automatic function that gently leans the car into corners like a motorcycle.

Advanced technology in the S-Class gives the sedan driver extra help behind the wheel. One system scans the road at 1,000 times per second to adjust for a controlled ride. Another system alerts the driver if the car drifts from its lane. The car can also park itself.

АЗБУКА
Х422ММ 197
Х018СТ 777

PASSENGER PAMPERING

The driver's seat feels like a personal cloud in the S-Class sedan. Almost 20 motors work to adjust the seat position for perfect comfort. Even the back seats recline with leg rests. They also massage and wrap each passenger in soothing heat.

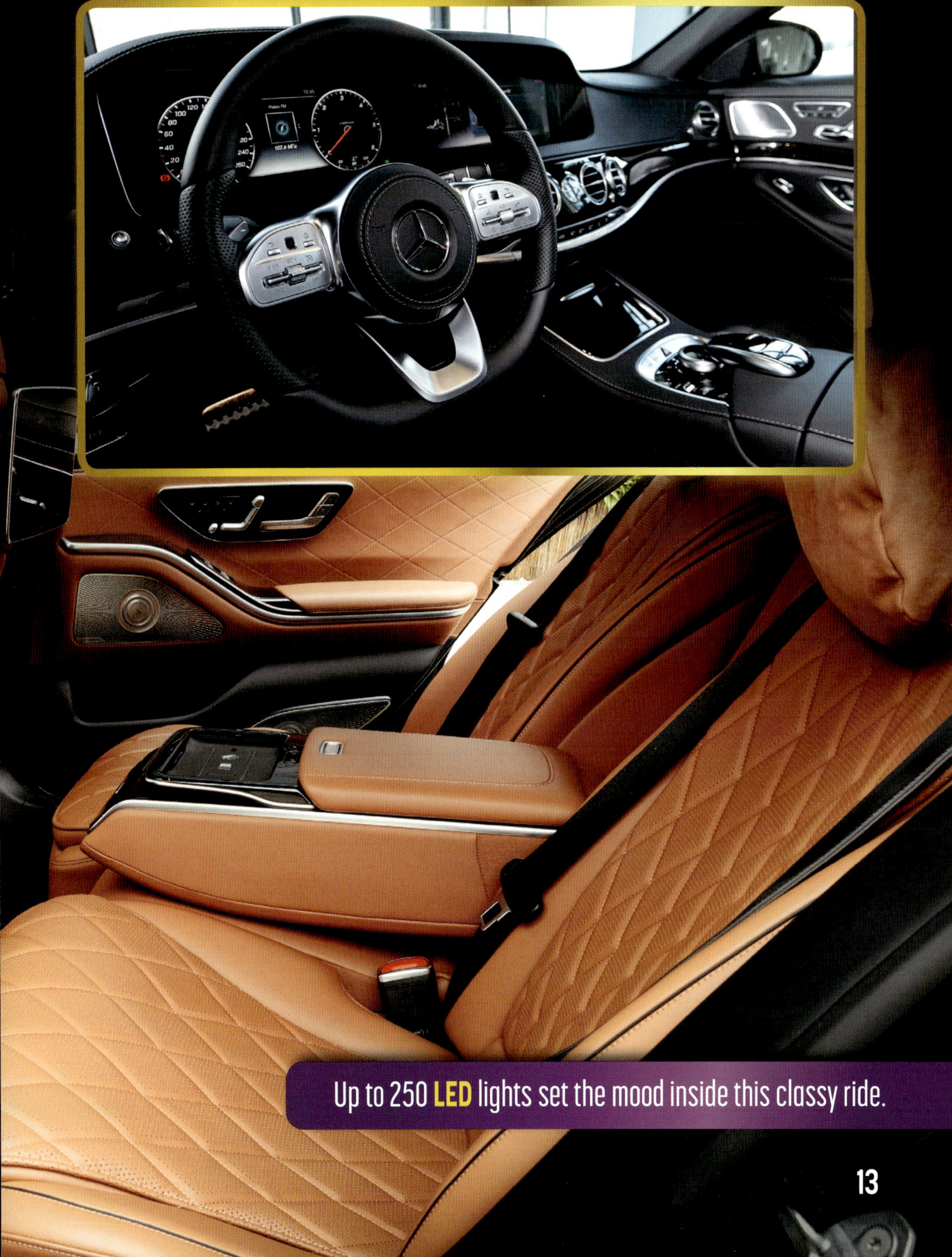

Up to 250 **LED** lights set the mood inside this classy ride.

Up to five screens deliver information and entertainment. The digital gauge cluster behind the steering wheel works with other onboard technology to create a three-dimensional effect on the huge center screen. **Navigation** arrows also project onto the front window. Twin rear-seat screens and an optional 22-speaker stereo system rock the cabin.

The sedan uses real-time eye tracking, facial recognition, and fingerprint scanning to adjust the car's systems to the driver and boost security.

POWERFUL CHOICES

Mercedes-Benz S-Class shoppers often choose between the S500 or S580 model. The motor is the main difference—and both deliver plenty of **horsepower**.

- S500: **Turbocharged** 3.0-liter six-cylinder engine for 429 horsepower
- S580: Twin-turbo 4.0-liter V-8 engine for 496 horsepower

Onboard electronics limit the S-Class cars' top speed in the U.S. to 130 mph (209 km/h).

The Mercedes-Benz Maybach S-Class S560 and S650 models attract **elite** owners. Maybachs are longer and A LOT fancier inside than other vehicles. They're also super-powered under the hood. The S650 launches like a rocket with a 6.0-liter V12 twin-turbo motor for 621 horsepower. It's pricier than most cars, too, starting above $200,000!

A speedster sedan, the Mercedes-Maybach flies from 0 to 60 mph (97 km/h) in just 4.6 seconds.

SERIOUS SAFETY

Mercedes-Benz built the first **crumple zone** in 1959 and the first airbag system in 1980 to protect passengers. Today's S-Class sedans lead the car industry with rear-seat airbags and a system that lifts the car in a crash to reduce impact.

Safe self-driving cars could be next for Mercedes-Benz. These cars handle slow and crowded highways, allowing the driver to pay less attention to the road while tending to business.

MBHK 3

FIRST IN FIRSTS

During its long history, Mercedes-Benz has earned a **reputation** for setting records on the racecourse. The company sponsored driver Ewy Rosqvist in 1962. She was the first woman to win the Argentinian Grand Prix. She also set a record for finishing three hours before anyone else.

Ewy Rosqvist (Right)

Many experts believe that the 1886 Benz Patent Motorwagen was the world's first automobile. Built by Karl Benz, his wife Bertha was the first driver.

Karl Benz

Bertha Benz

Today Mercedes-Benz wants to set the highest factory standards for reducing harmful effects on the environment. People matter, too. The company painted the words "End Racism" on each of its Silver Arrow racecars.

During the 2020 racing season, Mercedes-Benz urged fans to support including *everyone* in the sport, in business, and in life.

LOYALS EVERYWHERE

Mercedes-Benz operates 93 locations worldwide and is headquartered in Stuttgart, Germany. The S-Class luxury line continues to attract loyal customers everywhere. They expect the best or nothing!

In the U.S., 70 percent of Mercedes-Benz owners purchase the brand again for their next vehicle. They're loyal fans.

GLOSSARY

chrome (KROHM): Shiny silver metal used for protection or decoration

coupé (coo-PAY in Europe; COOP in the U.S.): A two-seat car with a sloped roof

crumple zone (KRUHM-puhl ZOHN): Part of a vehicle designed to absorb energy in a crash

elite (i-LEET or AY-leet): Very rich or important people

flagship (FLAG-ship): The leading or most important vehicle in a group

horsepower (HORS-pou-ur): A unit for measuring an engine's power

LED (EL-EE-DEE): Stands for "light-emitting diode," a type of light source

navigation (NAV-i-GAY-shuhn): Finding a location and providing directions to another

reputation (REP-yuh-TAY-shuhn): A judgment of someone or something

turbocharged (TUR-boh-CHARJD): Built with a device that pushes extra air into an engine for more power

INDEX

WEBSITES TO VISIT

https://www.dkfindout.com/us/transportation/history-cars/

https://www.caranddriver.com/mercedes-benz/s-class

https://carbuzz.com/cars/mercedes-benz/s-class/2021

ABOUT THE AUTHOR

Tracy Nelson Maurer

Tracy Nelson Maurer has written more than 100 nonfiction books for young readers. She lives in Minnesota where she happily drives a minivan.

Produced by: Blue Door Education for Crabtree Publishing

Written by: Tracy Nelson Maurer

Designed by: Jennifer Dydyk

Edited by: Kelli Hicks

Proofreader: Janine Deschenes

Photographs: Cover: Logo graphic © Shutterstock.com/officeku, speedometer © Shutterstock.com/Panuwatccn, shiny car hood top left and throughout book © Shutterstock.com/ Inked Pixels, Mercedes cover photo © Artzzz| Dreamstime.com, Title: ©Artzzz| Dreamstime.com, PG 4: ©Hanohiki| Dreamstime.com (top), ©Sergey Kohl| Dreamstime.com, PG 5: © filmfoto/istock.com (top), ©Grzegorz Czapski| Dreamstime.com, PG 6: ©Jack Skeens / Shutterstock.com, PG 7: © DoubleBoris / Shutterstock.com, PG 8: ©Artur_Nyk / Shutterstock.com (spread), © Stanislav Sablin/istock.com, PG 9: © AdrianHancu/istock.com (inset), PG 10: © Mike Mareen / Shutterstock.com (spread), © Tadeáš Skuhra| Dreamstime.com (inset), PG 11: © Konev Timur/istock.com (inset), PG 12-13: © Artur_Nyk / Shutterstock.com (spread), PG 13: ©Vitalij Sova| Dreamstime.com (inset), PG 14-15: ©Artur_Nyk / Shutterstock.com, PG 16: ©Timur Konev| Dreamstime.com, PG 17: ©Daimler AG. All Rights Reserved (all), PG 18-19: ©Daimler AG. All Rights Reserved (all), Kanye West photo © Editorial credit: Tinseltown / Shutterstock.com, PG 20: ©atlantic-kid/istock.com, PG 21: ©Daimler AG. All Rights Reserved (inset), ©AdrianHancu/istock.com, PG 22: ©Gabo_Arts / Shutterstock.com (spread), PG 23: Teddy Leung / Shutterstock.com (top), ©Konstantin Grigorev| Dreamstime.com, PG 24: ©Shyripa Alexandr / Shutterstock.com (bottom), ©Ewy_Rosqvist_Public Archives, PG 25: ©Daimler AG. All Rights Reserved (top), Benz Portraits public domain images, PG 26-27: ©Daimler AG. All Rights Reserved. Mercedes Benze Racing, PG 28: ©Tobias Arhelger / Shutterstock.com, PG 29: ©Teddyleung| Dreamstime.com (top), ©(null) (null)| Dreamstime.com

Library and Archives Canada Cataloguing in Publication

Title: S-Class by Mercedes-Benz / Tracy Nelson Maurer.
Names: Maurer, Tracy Nelson, 1965- author.
Description: Series statement: Luxury rides | "A Crabtree branches book". | Includes index.
Identifiers: Canadiana (print) 20210220627 | Canadiana (ebook) 20210220635 | ISBN 9781427154873 (hardcover) | ISBN 9781427154934 (softcover) | ISBN 9781427154996 (HTML) | ISBN 9781427155054 (EPUB) | ISBN 9781427155115 (read-along ebook)
Subjects: LCSH: Mercedes automobiles—Juvenile literature.

Classification: LCC TL215.M4 M38 2022 | DDC j629.222/2—dc23

Library of Congress Cataloging-in-Publication Data

Names: Maurer, Tracy Nelson, 1965- author.
Title: S-Class by Mercedes-Benz / Tracy Nelson Maurer.
Description: New York : Crabtree Publishing Company, [2022] | Series: Luxury rides | "A Crabtree branches book." | Includes bibliographical references and index.
Identifiers: LCCN 2021022144 (print) | LCCN 2021022145 (ebook) | ISBN 9781427154873 (hardcover) | ISBN 9781427154934 (paperback)| ISBN 9781427154996 (ebook) | ISBN 9781427155054 (epub) | ISBN 9781427155115
Subjects: LCSH: Mercedes automobiles--Juvenile literature.
Classification: LCC TL215.M4 M325 2022 (print) | LCC TL215.M4 (ebook) | DDC 629.222/2--dc23
LC record available at https://lccn.loc.gov/2021022144

LC ebook record available at https://lccn.loc.gov/2021022145

Crabtree Publishing Company

www.crabtreebooks.com 1-800-387-7650

Printed in the U.S.A./072021/CG20210514

Published in the United States
Crabtree Publishing
347 Fifth Avenue, Suite 1402-145
New York, NY, 10016

Published in Canada
Crabtree Publishing
616 Welland Ave.
St. Catharines, ON, L2M 5V6